Compendium of Trial Advocacy Drills

NITA Editorial Board

Compendium of Trial Advocacy Drills

Robert A. Stein

Ben Rubinowitz

National Institute for Trial Advocacy

Reproduction Permission
National Institute for Trial Advocacy
361 Centennial Parkway, Suite 220
Louisville, CO 80027
(800) 225-6482
http://www.nita.org

Stein, Robert A. and Ben Rubinowitz, *Compendium of Trial Advocacy Drills* (NITA, 2006).

ISBN-10: 1-55681-961-7
ISBN-13: 978-1-55681-961-2

Contents

Acknowledgments

The compilers wish to acknowledge the creative genius and energy of their colleagues throughout the Land of NITA, who have created, refined, and reinvented these drills. In particular, we want to thank the TOADS, Pat McCloskey, Dave Geneson, Bill Hunt, Patricia Williams, and Nancy Vaidik.

Watching a brilliant skier swoosh effortlessly down the slopes, a competitive swimmer glide through the water, or a gifted trial lawyer perform legal pirouettes is a joy to behold and a thing of beauty. Ask each of these performers how they do what they do, and you will probably get the answer *"I don't know, I just do."*

The burden on the teacher of advocacy is to break down the component parts of a brilliant examination, articulate what makes it a brilliant examination, reduce the brilliance to its specific parts, and then create methods of reproducing the skill so as to impart it to students. Further, advocacy teachers must acknowledge that some participants learn intellectually, others learn existentially, and still others learn simply by rote doing.

One of the most powerful teaching tools available to instructors of trial advocacy is the drills. Drills focus the participants' attention on mini-exercises designed to isolate and thereby enhance their knowledge of specific trial techniques. If done properly, drills bring a tremendous amount of energy to the classroom. Each participant in the class knows that he or she will be called on, in short order, to participate, and the drills become contagious as each participant becomes eager for his or her turn. The reviews of these drill sessions by participants have been unanimous: Not only do the participants love the format, but they continually want more.

In short, the enthusiasm generated by this format will make any advocacy training course even more successful.

Drills are portable. Once learned, drills can be used to introduce, master, and practice skills. The drills can also be used to resurrect skills that have been learned but lay dormant between trials.

The drills in this compendium are intended to be shared with anyone interested in teaching trial advocacy. While an unlimited number of drills can be used in any trial advocacy course, the drills presented here have been used successfully by the contributors to this compendium, many of whom have taught trial advocacy for decades. The contributors are of the firm belief that drills belong to no one and should be used by everyone.

❖ To break the ice.

❖ To increase the energy level of the class.

❖ To punctuate a point and/or reduce boredom during a lecture.

❖ To teach one skill through repetition and example.

❖ To have a participant deviate from a script and act on instinct, i.e., deal with surprise and think on his or her feet.

❖ To teach spontaneity and how to deal with the unexpected, e.g., the non-responsive witness.

❖ To engender consistent excellence in a participant's examination.

❖ To allow the participant to "feel" their way through a new skill or methodology until it becomes "imprinted" and becomes second nature.

❖ To force the participant to work without notes and overcome the fear of failure without them.

❖ To serve as a practice or warm-up tool in preparation for trial.

How Drills Work

Drills work best in small groups of no more than ten to twelve participants. In this setting an instructor can break the ice by working with the participants, individually or as a group, to enhance the energy level of everyone. Drills should be used as building blocks, beginning with relatively basic trial techniques to form the foundation for more sophisticated drills that teach complex skills. Drills work best, and attention levels are highest, when the participants know that they will be called upon to participate but cannot predict the order in which that participation will occur.

❖ Use drills incrementally and focus them at the skill level of the participants.

❖ Use drills to teach skills that can be learned through repetition.

❖ Use drills to teach skills that can be broken into component parts.

❖ Explain the purpose and objective of the drill to the participants before performing the drill.

❖ Give explicit and detailed instructions to participants and other faculty members before beginning.

❖ Give a mini-lecture, if necessary, on the skill being taught.

❖ Involve the entire class.

❖ Be patient with participants who need more time.

❖ Provide nonjudgmental correction to participants during the performance.

❖ Wrap up with concluding remarks about the lesson learned.

❖ Have everyone, including faculty, on their feet during the entire drill.

❖ Create a nonthreatening, fun atmosphere.

❖ Realize that performing a drill is a high-anxiety moment for each participant and use this constructively.

Drills

Drill 1
Volume, Pace, and Gestures

The Emphasis Drill

Purpose/Explanation

Teach participants how to use tonality, pause, and gesticulation to emphasize or de-emphasize words during an examination, opening statement, or closing argument.

A recurring problem in teaching advocacy is that beginning participants often speak in monotone coupled with a limp, expressionless body. This type of oration is about as exciting as watching your car rust, and has little chance to be memorable or persuasive. To break the participants of the monotonous mold, use this drill.

Level: Basic

Mechanics

Write a phrase on the board. It can be virtually anything declaratory. Examples are: "There are no fish under the ice" and "I never promised you the money." Any phrase will do, as long as there are possibilities for using gestures and it can be made into a question as well as a declaratory sentence. You will be manipulating the phrase in several ways.

Next, explain to the participants that this drill is designed to do away forever with boring speech. Tell them they will each get up and say the same sentence several times. Each time they say the sentence, however, they must emphasize a different word. Show them what you mean by demonstrating the drill. Start by emphasizing the word "I" in the following phrase, and show them what an appropriate hand gesture is at the same time by pointing to yourself.

"*I* never said I'd give you money."

Next, move on to the second word, "never," and again demonstrate an appropriate hand or head gesture while emphasizing that word orally.

"I *never* said I'd give you money."

"I never *said* I'd give you money."

The participants must go through the entire sentence, emphasizing a different word each time. We find that applauding after the participant completes the task gives the participant an immediate sense of accomplishment. It also brings smiles to the faces of everyone in the group because they realize that they are engaged in a beneficial exercise that has immediate results—one that requires personal investment. (In other words, they go next.)

Another variation of this drill requires participants to stand up in a group and repeat the phrase at different volumes. Begin with the group of participants reciting the phrase all together in a loud voice, increasing the volume to the level of shouting. Then have them repeat the phrase in lower modulations to the point of whispering. Next, divide the group in two. Ask one group to repeat the phrase at a loud volume; the other group in a whisper.

Now use further variations. Have each participant individually repeat the phrase, either shouting or whispering at the direction of the instructor. Next, have the group, *en masse*, repeat half the phrase with a three-second pause between some words, again at the instructor's direction. Next, ask the group to repeat the phrase with two pauses between two words that the instructor selects. Increase the length of time for the pauses. Have the participants, one by one, repeat the phrase with at least one pause of a three-, four-, or five-second duration, increasing the difficulty level so that there are one, two, or three pauses for two, three, four, or five seconds, on an *ad hoc* basis. Finally, have the group repeat the phrase with a whisper, a pause, and a shout, with each participant picking his or her own variation, producing a cacophony of noise. Then let each participant showcase his or her phrase with a pause, at high volume, and then at low volume.

Indeed, the majority of the participants will already have started using hand gestures automatically. Now have the group practice the same phrase using a hand gesture. (*Caveat*: the hand gesture you choose should be consistent with the emphasis or de-emphasis.) Each participant in turn delivers the phrase emphasized with an appropriate hand gesture.

Now comes the big one: Direct the entire group in practicing the phrase with a pause, a hand gesture, a whisper, and at high volume. Then each individual delivers his or her own pause, gesture, whisper, and high volume combination. Finally, divide the group in half. Have a person from one group start by delivering the phrase with maximum emphasis, including hand gestures, pauses, and changes in volume. Ask a person from the second group to respond. Repeat the drill with all participants performing in responsive pairs, with each person speaking the same phrase.

Drill 2
Direct Examination

The Who, What, When, Where Drill

Purpose/Explanation

Teach participants to ask direct-examination questions that call for a descriptive answer. This drill helps participants learn to conduct a proper direct examination without sustaining objection.

Level: Basic

Mechanics

Make up an easy-to-understand story, such as a robbery that occurred while you were walking to work. You play the parts of the witness *and* the judge. Tell the participants a minimum number of facts—e.g., something happened to you on June 12, one year ago, at 12:00 noon. Have them find out the entire factual scenario by asking questions using the Who, What, When, Where, How, Why, Describe, Explain, and Elaborate format. Give each participant an opportunity to ask only one or two questions before moving to the next participant. Remind the participants that they should not move on from a specific subject area (e.g., a detailed description of the robber) until they have enough information to sum up effectively on that point. If they start a question that calls for a "yes" or "no" response, sustain an objection based on leading. Also sustain objections for questions that begin with verbs such as: Did, Didn't, Were, Weren't, Could, Couldn't, Should, Shouldn't, Have, Haven't, So, etc. Continue until each participant understands how to ask objection-proof questions. As things progress, you can use this same format to teach the "double direct" or "looping" technique (see Drill 3).

Drill 3
Direct Examination

The Double Direct/Looping Drill

Purpose/Explanation

Teach participants the art of looping back, i.e., repeating in the next question an important portion of the answer formerly elicited. Double direct, or looping, allows the examiner to emphasize the most important part of a crucial answer by repeating a portion of that answer in the next question.

It is important to be aware that looping has its limitations. Looping should be saved for the most important testimony, because a question that loops back is technically argumentative: It is asked not for the purpose of eliciting information, but to emphasize or argue facts to the jury. In addition, a lawyer who habitually loops back creates a boring and monotonous examination. That being said, the technique can be very effective.

Level: Basic/Intermediate

Mechanics

In this drill, you play the witness. Have the first participant ask a direct-examination question, which you answer. Then have the next participant use part of your answer in the next direct-examination question (i.e., the participant must "loop back").

For example, using Drill 2's robbery case, a participant may ask you:

> **Q:** What did he do at that time?
>
> **A:** He pulled out a knife.

Invariably, the next participant will ask:

> **Q:** What happened next?

Show the participants how to emphasize the drama of the events by using the double direct format:

> **Q:** When the defendant pulled out the knife, what happened?

or

> **Q:** When the defendant pulled out the knife, what did *he* do?

or

> **Q:** When the defendant pulled out the knife, what did *you* do?

or

> **Q:** When the defendant pulled out the knife, what were you thinking?

It is important to remind the participants that looping back can be used to highlight certain important areas but ought not to be used for every question with every witness.

Drill 4
Direct and/or Cross-Examination

The One-Fact-per-Question Drill

Purpose/Explanation

Teach participants how to ask questions that convey one thought or fact per question by using simple words.

Level: Basic

Mechanics

Stand in the front of the room and have the participants ask a series of nonleading questions to elicit a description of your clothing. Each participant, in turn, must ask a question in direct-examination style, with Who, What, When, Where, Why, Describe, Explain, etc., as the preface, using ten words or less. It works best if one instructor monitors whether the questions are in direct style while a second instructor monitors the number of words. As the participants start to figure out the drill, have them use fewer words—eight words or less, then five words, and then three. This drill can also be used as a simple cross-examination drill using questions in cross-examination style.

Drill 5
Direct Examination

The Picture-Drawing Drill

Purpose/Explanation

Teach participants how to set a descriptive scene during direct-examination questioning.

Level: Basic

Mechanics

Ask each participant to draw a picture of something. Then have the participants pair up and describe to each other what they have drawn. Next, ask the participants to stand up. Have one member of each pair lead the other through a direct examination about his or her picture. Then have the participants change roles, with the other member of the pair conducting the examination. The whole room will be filled with noise as the participants learn to describe a series of marks on paper to lead their partners to the conclusion that a picture of a particular object has been drawn (e.g., a cat or a house). Ask some of the participant pairs to showcase their performances.

Drill 6
Cross-Examination

The Freeze-Frame Technique

Purpose/Explanation

Although life moves quickly, it can be thought of as nothing more than an infinite series of frames, strung together in the same manner as an illustrator creates a series of cells for a cartoon. To maximize the impact of any quickly evolving event, the trial lawyer should attempt to break the event down into multiple snapshots, revealing all of the emotions, thoughts, and actions that make up one short period of time.

Teach participants to use the "freeze-frame" approach to develop a point, emphasize it, and make the importance of that point unmistakably clear to the jury.

In every trial there are facts that must be presented to develop the strong points of the case. Proper emphasis on these facts at various stages in the trial can work to support the advocate's position during final argument.

Level: Intermediate (Cross); Advanced (Direct)

The purpose of the drill is to practice cross-examination skills independent of a fact pattern related to a case. The aim is for the participants to ask only leading questions, and to expand the time and importance of the subject matter being inquired through multiple leading questions, one fact at a time.

The Pen Drill (Cross)

While standing at the front of the classroom, reach into your pocket, withdraw a pen, and drop it on the floor. Advise the participants to watch you closely. Now, direct the participants to cross-examine on the act they have just observed.

Have the participants ask a minimum of ten to twelve questions on the event, making a relatively quick act seem like a long process. A single leading question such as "you dropped your pen, didn't you?" is not the aim. Rather, the participants should be encouraged to start small and stay small (e.g., "Your hand was at your side? You began to lift it? You lifted it all the way to your chest level? Once there, you put it inside? Inside your coat, you have a pocket? That pocket is on the left-hand inside portion of the lining? You put your hand in there, correct?" etc.) The drill continues until the pen is taken from the pocket, released, and hits the floor. The drill can be expanded by introducing notions of intent, motive, *mens rea*, time, etc. (e.g., "You wanted to let it slip from your fingers?"). Looping of answers to questions (i.e., beginning a question by repeating a portion of the previous answer) can also be emphasized as well as changing the tone of one's voice for emphasis.

The Pen with Theme Drill (Direct or Cross)

This drill takes The Pen Drill, described previously, a step further. Begin by having the participants perform The Pen Drill, using either cross- or direct examination. Have the participants ask questions that take the pen from the pocket and down to the floor in the slowest possible way. Now, repeat the same drill, but this time make the pen a bomb. Insist that the participants ask not only about the physical movements of the pen/bomb through space, but also what the witness was thinking as he or she was moving the pen/bomb, to wit, "You were scared. You were shaking. You thought you were going to die. You were relieved."

Finally, have the participants do the same drill for a third time, but this time ask the participants to suggest a theme that will be emphasized throughout the examination (e.g., "Your heart was pounding"). Ask the person who comes up with the theme to repeat it every third or fourth question (e.g., "Your heart was pounding," or "Your life passed before your eyes").

Drill 7
Cross-Examination

The Eraser Drill

Purpose/Explanation

This is a variation of The Pen Drill. The aim of The Eraser Drill, as with The Pen Drill, is to require participants to ask leading questions, change their tone of voice as they proceed, and inquire about a specific point in time.

Level: Intermediate

Mechanics

Walk to the front of the class, pick up an eraser, and throw it across the room so that it hits a wall. Direct the participants to conduct an immediate cross-examination of everything they observed by utilizing the freeze-frame technique. Permit each participant to ask three or four questions and then choose another participant at random to continue the drill.

Voice and tone drills can be conducted throughout the exercise. Have the participants ask the same question more than once using different word emphasis, a pause for greater emphasis, or a different hand gesture to allow for better advocacy.

Drill 8
Cross-Examination

The Using-Operative-Words Drill

Purpose/Explanation

Teach participants the value of using operative words from the court's instruction during cross-examination.

While it is understood that attorneys may not instruct the jurors on the law in the midst of cross-examination, it is advantageous to use some of the operative words or terms from the court's anticipated instruction to support final argument. The use of such operative words allows the attorney to use terms or words which will later be spoken by the court. If done properly, the jury will think that the attorney came up with these operative words and that the court was merely taking its lead from the attorney.

Level: Advanced

Mechanics

Take the same factual scenario used in the robbery example (see Drill 2). This time, however, write the words "conscious objective" or "intent" on the blackboard. Tell the participants that these words are right out of the court's charge. The goal is for the participants to work these words into their cross examination.

For example:

> **Q:** It was your conscious objective to reach for the gun, true?
>
> **Q:** It was your conscious objective to point the gun at his face, correct?
>
> **Q:** It was your intent to take the money, right?

This same drill can be used with virtually any type of case. For example, take a medical malpractice example and write the words "departure from accepted standards of care." Tell the participants a doctor failed to take the patient's temperature. The goal of questioning is to end up with the question:

> **Q:** You would agree with me that the failure to take the patient's temperature was a departure from accepted standards of medical care, true?

Drill 9
Object Examination

The Schizophrenia Drill

Purpose/Explanation

Teach participants the value of asking a series of short, one-fact questions leading to a final conclusion that the witness cannot dispute. This is also known as cross-examining objects or The Schizophrenia Drill.

Level: Intermediate

Mechanics

Ask each participant to hold an object (e.g., a water bottle) in his or her hand, and to then cross-examine that object. The drill proceeds whereby the characteristics of the water bottle are elicited by the examiner. Only at the end of the examination does the examiner announce that the object is a water bottle. For example, "You are six inches tall. You are made of plastic. You have a label. The label is green and located on your exterior. The label says Poland Springs. There is a sloshing sound when you are moved up and down. You are purchased by me. You are a water bottle."

Drill 10
Cross-/Direct Examination

The Tennis Ball Drill

Purpose/Explanation

Teach participants to keep their eyes and ears focused on the witness instead of concentrating on their notes.

Level: Intermediate

Mechanics

Explain to the participants that the only time words can be exchanged in the drill is when someone is holding a tennis ball. Begin by asking a participant to hold a tennis ball while asking questions of a witness in a preassigned examination. After each question is asked, the participant is to toss the tennis ball to the witness. The witness then answers the question. Anytime the examiner diverts his or her eyes from the witness by looking away or down at notes, the witness is authorized to throw the ball at the examiner. Participants should be instructed to throw the ball away from the examiner's face or other sensitive areas. When the witness is done answering each question, the tennis ball is tossed back into the hands of the examiner.

Drill 11
Cross-/Direct Examination

The Ultimate Question Drill

Purpose/Explanation

Teach participants to ask a sufficient number of questions that allows the examiner to ask the ultimate question on direct or cross-examination.

Level: Intermediate;
Advanced if participants are not allowed to take or use notes

Mechanics

Ask the participants to visualize their most embarrassing experience (not their saddest, but their most embarrassing or humiliating) and their funniest experience. (You can also use other experiences, such as their best vacation.) Then have the participants pair up and interview each other. One partner should relate a most embarrassing experience and the other partner should relate a funniest experience.

After the interview, each partner should examine the other partner using direct or cross-examination rules. For instance, the first partner would do a direct examination on what has just been elicited as the second partner's funniest experience. Then the second partner would cross-examine the first partner on his or her most embarrassing experience. All the examinations must be done in proper form with one thought per question. (For example, direct examination questions must begin with Who, What, Where, When, Why, How, Describe, Show, Tell, or Explain.) Only when the entirety of the information elicited in the initial interview is "on the record" may the cross-examiner ask the ultimate question: "And that was your most embarrassing experience?" Similarly, the direct examiner earns the right to ask of the witness, "Please describe how you felt about this experience." The goal is to elicit a corresponding answer such as: "It was the funniest experience of my life," "It was the most embarrassing experience of my life," "It was the best vacation of my life."

Drill 12
Advanced Direct/Cross-Examination

The Thinking-on-Your-Feet Drill

Purpose/Explanation

Teach participants how to think critically on the spot in the courtroom. The objective is to have the participants respond immediately to a new set of circumstances and be able to ask either a direct or cross-examination follow-up.

Level: Advanced

Mechanics

Create a scenario for examination using a common object. Have the participants seated in rows. Hand one participant an object with multiple characteristics, such as a set of car keys, a book, a purse, or a wallet. Ask the first person who takes the object to identify one characteristic of the item (e.g., "The wallet is leather"). The next person takes the wallet in hand and asks the prior person a direct-examination question about the wallet (e.g., "What is this material?"). The next person in line asks a cross-examination question about the identical topic (e.g., "This is leather, isn't it?"). This continues along the row with a characteristic being identified by one participant, the next doing a direct examination on that characteristic, and the next doing a cross. The point is to make the direct relate to the cross, and to show that any direct can be turned into cross and vice-versa. You can also do this drill by identifying the characteristic yourself and then having each participant to do first a direct and then a cross.

Drill 13
Evidentiary Foundations/Direct Examination

The Conga Line Drill

Purpose/Explanation

Teach participants how to introduce exhibits and lay persuasive evidentiary foundations. The purpose of this drill is to make the learning of evidentiary foundations fun and easy. The drill relies on the principle of memory muscle.

Level: Intermediate

Mechanics

Ask the participants to stand in line before a witness with an item of evidence that is to be marked and offered. The first person in line asks a question regarding foundations. Once the question is asked, *briefly* critique the participant and have him or her ask the question again and again until perfect. Have the rest of the participants, in turn, do the same thing with respect to different foundational elements (identification, authentication, relevance, hearsay, etc.). By the time the line reaches the fourth or fifth participant, the item should be in evidence.

Repeat the drill with the next participant in line, using another piece of evidence. As the participants at the back of the line repeatedly hear the drill for laying a proper foundation, it becomes embedded in their memory. The drill works best if the instructor keeps the line moving quickly, without pausing for an extended critique, mini-lecture, or demonstration. It is also helpful to write the acronym MSGLOU (Mark, Show, Give, Lay foundation, Offer, Use) on the board to remind everyone of the process.

Variation 1: Photograph

Assume the same set of facts as earlier (i.e., the robbery scenario). Use a large photograph of a specific location and tell the group that this is the location of the robbery. The drill is formulated to force the participants first to set the scene through direct examination; second, to introduce the exhibit in evidence; and third, to mark the exhibit so that it can be used appropriately on summation. A participant who misses a step must return to the end of the line.

You can perform this drill using any large photograph with a corresponding story. Have the participants conduct an objection-proof direct examination and then work with the exhibit.

Variation 2: Knife (real evidence)

Use the same format as above and build on the original story. Explain that the police arrested the robber two blocks away and discovered the knife. Assume the police officer labeled the knife with an evidence tag bearing the date and his signature. Ask the participants to introduce the knife in evidence.

Drill 14
Chain of Custody

The Visualization Drill

Purpose/Explanation

Teach the participants to lay a foundation based on chain of custody by visualizing what happened to a particular object.

Level: Intermediate

Mechanics

Have the participants visualize and describe a chain-of-custody scenario. For example, you could use a drug confiscation fact pattern. Have the participants visualize cocaine being confiscated from a female suspect's bra into a police officer's hands, traveling from the scene of the arrest to the lab, being put in various plastic baggies, being labeled, being handled at the lab, being tested, and then being brought to the courtroom. Have the participants pretend they are a genie in the cocaine bag, and have them talk about their trip. Once the participants have talked about their trip, have them work in pairs. Ask each participant to write down a description of the trip, and then conduct a direct examination of their partner about the trip.

Drill 15
Objections

The No-Speeches Drill

Purpose/Explanation

Teach participants the art of making an effective objection without making speeches or speaking objections. This drill is designed to teach participants to recognize that certain questions proffered by the examiner are objectionable. It is also designed to help them state the specific basis for the objection (e.g., leading, asked and answered, assuming facts in evidence, etc.).

Level: Basic to Intermediate

Mechanics

Ask each participant to stand and make an objection based on a direct-examination scenario performed by you or another instructor. Do not permit seated objections. Direct the participants to make their objections briefly and crisply (e.g., "Objection, hearsay," or "Objection, leading," or "Objection, foundation"). The drill moves quickly, and an entire classroom can be covered in three to five minutes. Participants are directed to repeat the correct phraseology. The drill works best if sprung on the class in the midst of an examination rather than prepared for in advance.

One way of conducting this drill is to explain to the group that you are bringing in a talented and experienced lawyer to demonstrate the proper way to conduct a direct examination. Don't tell the participants this is an objections drill. Instead, let them think it's an important demonstration. Tell them that you will play the part of the witness, introduce the demonstrating lawyer, and, as an aside, mention that if something is objectionable they can object. *What they won't know is that virtually the entire direct examination will be objectionable*. If the participants don't catch on immediately, press the absurdity to the next level. For example, start the direct examination:

> **Q:** You're a police officer?
>
> **Q:** You've been a police officer for fifteen years?
>
> **Q:** You're an expert in your field?
>
> **Q:** Capable of determining the guilt or innocence of perpetrators, true?

Hopefully, the participants have caught on by now. Continue the direct until the participants are routinely stating the proper basis of the objection:

> **Q:** Tell us exactly what the defendant was thinking at the time you arrested him.
>
> **Q:** Tell us exactly what you were thinking at that time.
>
> **Q:** What did the slime-bag do next?
>
> **Q:** He was properly advised of his rights, true?

Q: Your boss knew he was guilty, true?

Q: Without telling us what your boss said, tell us the words he used in describing the defendant.

Q: Approach the board and draw a fair and accurate diagram of the crime scene.

Q: Please mark on the diagram a "G" for guilty where the robbery took place.

Drill 16
Impeachment

The Confirm, Clue, Credit, Confront Drill

Purpose/Explanation

Teach participants to impeach a witness using a prior inconsistent statement. The examiner's objective is to persuade the jury that the prior statement is true.

Level: Basic

Mechanics

Present a traffic accident scenario. The witness role is played by you or another faculty member. Explain that the witness has testified on direct that the light was red, but at an earlier deposition the witness testified that the light was green. Begin by asking the first participant to confirm the direct-examination testimony. The participant may choose the old style, to wit, "You're not really saying the light was red?" or "Are you really claiming the light was red?"or the participant may choose the modern approach, "The light was green," or "The truth is, the light was green." In each instance, the witness sticks to the testimony given on direct examination.

Next, instruct the next participant on the "clue." "You and I have talked about this before," or "This isn't the first time you've been asked about the color of the light."

Next, go to the next participant to ask the creditation question, e.g., "You gave a deposition; it was at my office." Write the creditation point on the board. Continue the creditation process by having each participant ask a question (e.g., "You were with your lawyer"). Write a list of all the creditation points elicited by the participants on the board. Finally, ask each participant to confront the witness using one, two, or three of the creditation points. For example:

- "Mr. Witness, turning to your truthful deposition given three weeks ago, you said the light was green."
- "Mr. Witness, turning to your deposition given in my office with your lawyer present, you said the light was green."
- "Mr. Witness, turning to your truthful deposition at which you swore to tell the truth, your attorney was present, and you knew the importance of the event, you said the light was green."

In other words, get the participants to piggyback on the creditation and enhance the importance of the deposition, making it the Holy Grail. Do the same thing for a signed and notarized statement, a signed statement, an unsigned statement, or police report.

Drill 17
Opening Statement

The Using-Operative-Legal-Terms Drill

Purpose/Explanation

Teach participants the benefits of using certain operative terms in the opening statement.

Level: Advanced

Mechanics

Have each participant, in turn, present an opening statement concerning a simple car accident case. Inform the participants that the jury instruction reads as follows: "A driver is required to keep a reasonable and proper lookout and he or she should use that degree of care under the existing circumstances." Next, ask the participants to assume a motorist passed a stop sign without stopping. Have each participant weave certain operative terms into his or her opening. For example: "It was at this time that (the driver) approached the stop sign. It was at this time that he failed to keep a reasonable and proper lookout. It was at this time that he entered the intersection without ever stopping."

Drill 18
Closing Argument

The Relating-Cross-Exam-Questions-to-Closing Drill

Purpose/Explanation

Teach participants how to tie their cross-examination questions to their theory in closing argument.

Level: Intermediate

Mechanics

Ask each participant to prepare and present a cross-examination lasting no more than two minutes. At the end of each examination, have the participant argue to the jury the points just elicited on cross.

Drill 19
Closing Argument/Damages

The Money-Request Drill

Purpose/Explanation

Help participants become comfortable with requesting a monetary award during closing argument.

Level: Intermediate

Mechanics

Use this drill in the course of a mock closing argument. Have one participant stand up and say "I want money." Have another participant reply "You can't have it!" Then have the participants try multiple nuances on this concept. For example, the third participant says, "Give me the money!" and the fourth participant has to reply. The fifth participant then says, "Money, money, money!" and the sixth participant has to reply, "No, no, no!" Have the participants continue to argue about money: when they are entitled to money, and the appropriate responses as to why they are not entitled to it. It is similar to The Argument Drill, except based solely on the premise of money.

Drill 20
Closing Argument

The 3 x 5″ Index Card Drill

Purpose/Explanation

Teach the participants to synthesize an argument to the point of evolving a theme.

Level: Intermediate

Mechanics

Have each participant do a homework assignment, writing their entire case on one sheet of a legal pad before the training session begins. At the session, have the participants reduce their legal-pad notes to half of a page of paper. Then pass out a 3 x 5″ card and have them reduce their notes to the card. Have the participants continue to shrink the size of the note-keeping vehicle until it contains only one sentence, thereby distilling the essence of their argument. (The first participant to put his or her closing on a Post-it wins.)

Drill 21
Closing Argument/Opening Statement

The One-Minute Drill

Purpose/Explanation

Teach participants to argue or state their most persuasive facts up-front by shortening and synthesizing their argument or statement.

Level: Intermediate

Mechanics

This is essentially the same as The 3 x 5″ Card Drill (Drill 20) except the participants are asked to deliver the first minute of an opening or closing address. Provide each participant feedback on his or her ability to articulate a clear and persuasive theme. Have each participant progressively shorten the presentation to one minute, to thirty seconds, and finally to one sentence.

Drill 22
Closing Argument

The Argument v. Reciting Facts Drill

Purpose/Explanation

Teach the participants to argue the logical inferences from the facts during closing argument instead of merely reciting the facts.

Level: Advanced

Mechanics

Have the participants give closing arguments, which will probably sound more like statements. Next have them line up on one side of the room in pairs according to parties. Have the first participant give a one-sentence argument on the part of his or her case. Have the next participant rebut that specific argument. Continue down the line with the other participants. Permit one sentence per participant or a string of sentences, so long as the participants are using pure arguments.

> **For example:** Arthur Jackson never knew about George Avery's background.
>
> **Response:** Arthur Jackson is a liar.
>
> **Counter-response:** Where is the evidence that shows Arthur Jackson is a liar?

Response: His demeanor and the fact that he is an unscrupulous dog.

Response: The affair is a red herring, brought by the insurance company to avoid an obligation.

Make sure it is a pure argument, and go down the line so each participant gets a shot at the argument.

Drill 23
Closing Argument

Purpose/Explanation

To get the participants to react, argue, and be creative.

Level: Advanced

Mechanics

Line up in subgroups by party. Have the participants face one another and look at one another.

The first part of the drill is point/counterpoint. Have one of the plaintiffs argue one of the points of his or her case. Have the defendant respond, then proceed back and forth, going down the row so that everyone is called upon.

Next, use the question-and-answer technique. Have the plaintiff ask a question and require one of the defendant participants to respond. Again, go back and forth, alternating Q and A so that everyone gets to ask a question and everyone has to respond to a question that is asked.

Next, have the participants use an analogy or metaphor. Whoever comes up with the first one gets to raise it and see if the opposing party can respond. Continue back and forth until everyone has come up with some analogy or metaphor to put on the table.

Next, have participants argue credibility. For example, "Arthur Jackson is a liar," responded to with, "No, he isn't," or some other similar statement. Have participants argue why someone should or should not be believed. In short, have a structured argument that goes back and forth between the two warring sides.

Conclusion

Drills are fun, progressive, and by repetition serve to ingrain in the participants good habits and correct methods.

These drills should be used as an adjunct to the traditional NITA teaching—they are portable and give the participants a methodology by which they can refresh their skills before trial.